LARGEST CORPORATE
FRAUDS IN THE RECENT
HISTORY

SLEIGHT

SAHIL A GOSALIA

Cover design by Sahil A Gosalia

Published by: Independently Published

Disclaimer

The information presented in this book is for educational and informational purposes only. The author and publisher do not offer any legal, financial, or professional advice. The reader assumes all responsibility for any actions they take based on the information presented in this book. The author and publisher do not guarantee the accuracy or completeness of the information presented in this book. Any reliance the reader places on such information is strictly at their own risk. The author and publisher shall not be liable for any loss or damage, including but not limited to special, indirect, consequential, or incidental damages arising out of or in connection with the use or misuse of this book.

Foreword

The world of business is often seen as a cut-throat environment, where companies and individuals strive to be the best at any cost. Unfortunately, this drive for success can sometimes lead to unethical and even illegal practices, resulting in corporate frauds that can have devastating consequences.

In this book, "Sleight," the author takes us on a journey through some of the most significant corporate frauds of the 21st century. From Enron to Wirecard, the author presents a detailed account of each scandal, revealing the intricate web of lies and deceit that was woven by the perpetrators.

Through meticulous research and a deep understanding of the intricacies of corporate fraud, the author provides readers with an insightful look into the motivations behind each scheme and the devastating effects they had on the individuals and communities affected.

While each fraud is unique in its own way, the author has woven a common thread throughout the book: the importance of transparency, honesty, and ethical behavior in the corporate world. By shining a light on these egregious acts, the author reminds us of the critical role that accountability and integrity play in building and maintaining trust in the business community.

As you embark on this journey through the dark world of corporate fraud, I urge you to keep an open mind and to learn from the lessons presented in each chapter. By doing so, we can work towards creating a brighter future for businesses and communities alike, where honesty, transparency, and ethical behavior are valued above all else.

Sahil A Gosalia

Author

Dedication

"Dedicated to all the whistleblowers, journalists, and investigators who have tirelessly exposed the truth behind corporate fraud, shining a light on the dark corners of the business world and holding those in power accountable for their actions. Your courage and commitment to integrity inspire us all to demand a better, more transparent future for all."

Introduction

Corporate fraud is a shadowy, complicated world that often remains hidden from public view. Yet, its impact can be devastating, from destroying lives to shaking entire economies. In "Sleight," we delve into some of the biggest and most notorious corporate frauds of the 21st century.

Through meticulous research and analysis, we uncover the intricate schemes and tactics used by those who sought to deceive and defraud their stakeholders, employees, and investors. From Enron to Wirecard, we examine the consequences of their actions and the ripple effects they caused.

But "Sleight" is not just a book about the dark side of business. It is also a celebration of the brave individuals who stood up to these corporate giants and risked their careers and livelihoods to expose the truth. It is a tribute to the journalists, investigators, and whistleblowers who fought tirelessly to bring these frauds to light and to hold those in power accountable.

As you delve into the pages of "Sleight," I encourage you to approach these stories with an open mind and a critical eye. Through understanding the complexities of corporate fraud, we can begin to demand greater accountability, transparency, and ethical practices from those who hold power in the world of business.

I invite you to join me on this journey of discovery and exploration into the murky world of corporate fraud.

Table of Contents

1. **Enron**: The energy company filed for bankruptcy in 2001 due to fraudulent accounting practices.

2. **WorldCom**: In 2002, the telecommunications giant was exposed for $3.8 billion in accounting fraud.

3. **Tyco International:** The company's CEO, Dennis Kozlowski, was convicted in 2005 for stealing $600 million from the company.

4. **Bernie Madoff:** The former chairman of NASDAQ was exposed in 2008 for running the biggest Ponzi scheme in history, totalling $65 billion.

5. **HealthSouth:** The healthcare company was caught in a $2.7 billion accounting fraud scandal in 2003.

6. **Adelphia Communications**: The cable television company's founder and CEO were convicted in 2005 for stealing $2.3 billion from the company.

7. **Satyam Computer Services:** India's fourth-largest software company was exposed in 2009 for $1.5 billion in accounting fraud.

8. **Parmalat:** The Italian dairy and food company filed for bankruptcy in 2003 after it was discovered that they had falsified their accounts by over $14 billion.

9. **AIG**: The insurance company was bailed out by the US government in 2008 after it was revealed that it had engaged in fraudulent accounting practices.

10. **Olympus**: The Japanese camera and medical equipment manufacturer was exposed in 2011 for $1.7 billion in accounting fraud.

11. **Volkswagen**: The car manufacturer was caught in 2015 for cheating on emissions tests in over 11 million vehicles worldwide.

12. **Wells Fargo:** The bank was exposed in 2016 for opening millions of fake customer accounts without their knowledge or consent.

13. **Petrobras:** The Brazilian state-run oil company was involved in a $2 billion bribery and money laundering scandal in 2014.

14. **Toshiba**: The Japanese electronics company was caught in 2015 for overstating its profits by $1.2 billion over a period of seven years.

15. **Barclays**: The British bank was fined $450 million in 2012 for manipulating the LIBOR (London Interbank Offered Rate).

16. **Royal Bank of Scotland**: The bank was fined $610 million in 2013 for manipulating foreign exchange rates.

17. **Tesco**: The British supermarket chain was exposed in 2014 for overstating its profits by $400 million.

18. **Kobe Steel:** The Japanese steelmaker was caught in 2017 for falsifying data on the quality of its products.

19. **Steinhoff International:** The South African retailer was exposed in 2017 for inflating its profits by $7 billion over several years.

20. **Wirecard**: The German payment processor filed for bankruptcy in 2020 after it was discovered that it had engaged in fraudulent accounting practices, overstating its revenue and profits by billions of euros.

ONE

Enron

Enron was an American energy company that was once considered one of the largest and most innovative corporations in the world. However, in 2001, the company filed for bankruptcy, and it was revealed that the company had engaged in massive accounting fraud.

The fraud at Enron began in the 1990s when the company started using special-purpose entities (SPEs) to hide debt and inflate earnings. Enron executives would transfer the debt to these SPEs, which were off the company's balance sheet, to make it appear as if the company was more profitable than it actually was. This allowed Enron to maintain its credit rating, which was crucial for the company's continued growth.

Enron executives also used mark-to-market accounting, which allowed the company to record projected future profits as current revenue. This gave the impression that Enron was making more money than it actually was. The company also engaged in insider trading, whereby executives sold their Enron shares before the company's true financial position was revealed.

The fraud at Enron was finally exposed in 2001, when it was discovered that the company had overstated its earnings by more than $1 billion over several years. The company's stock price plummeted, and it was forced to file for bankruptcy. The scandal had far-reaching consequences, with thousands of employees losing their jobs and pensions, and investors losing billions of dollars.

In the aftermath of the Enron scandal, several executives were indicted and convicted, including CEO Jeffrey Skilling, who was sentenced to 24 years in prison, and former chairman Kenneth Lay, who died before he could be sentenced. The accounting firm Arthur Andersen, which had audited Enron's books, was also implicated in the fraud and was forced to dissolve.

The Enron scandal highlighted the need for stronger corporate governance and accounting standards. The Sarbanes-Oxley Act, which was passed in 2002, introduced stricter regulations for public companies and their auditors to prevent accounting fraud.

Specifics of Enron fraud:

- Enron executives used special-purpose entities (SPEs) to hide debt and inflate earnings.
- Mark-to-market accounting was used to record projected future profits as current revenue.
- Enron executives engaged in insider trading by selling their shares before their true financial position was revealed.
- Enron overstated its earnings by more than $1 billion over several years.
- The scandal led to the bankruptcy of Enron, the conviction of several executives, and the dissolution of the accounting firm Arthur Andersen.
- The Sarbanes-Oxley Act was introduced to prevent accounting fraud in public companies.

T W O

WorldCom

WorldCom was a telecommunications company that was once one of the largest companies in the United States. However, in 2002, the company was exposed for engaging in massive accounting fraud, which resulted in the company's bankruptcy.

The fraud at WorldCom was perpetrated by senior executives, who engaged in a scheme to inflate the company's earnings and hide its expenses. They did this by classifying normal operating expenses as capital expenditures, which allowed them to spread the costs over several years instead of recognizing them in the year in which they were incurred. This practice inflated the company's earnings and gave the impression that WorldCom was more profitable than it actually was.

The fraud was uncovered by an internal auditor, who discovered irregularities in the company's accounting records. When the auditor reported the findings to senior management, they were ignored, and the fraud continued. It was only when the Securities and Exchange Commission (SEC) launched an investigation that the full extent of the fraud was revealed.

The fallout from the WorldCom scandal was significant. Thousands of employees lost their jobs, and investors lost billions of dollars. The scandal also had a broader impact on the stock market and the telecommunications industry as a whole.

In the aftermath of the scandal, several executives were indicted and convicted, including CEO Bernard Ebbers, who was sentenced to 25 years in prison. The accounting firm Arthur Andersen, which had audited WorldCom's books, was also implicated in the fraud and was forced to dissolve.

The WorldCom scandal led to calls for greater transparency and accountability in corporate governance and accounting practices. It also resulted in the passage of the Sarbanes-Oxley Act, which introduced stricter regulations for public companies and their auditors to prevent accounting fraud.

Specifics of WorldCom fraud:

- Senior executives engaged in a scheme to inflate the company's earnings and hide its expenses.
- Normal operating expenses were classified as capital expenditures to spread the costs over several years instead of recognizing them in the year in which they were incurred.
- An internal auditor uncovered irregularities in the company's accounting records, which were ignored by senior management.
- The Securities and Exchange Commission (SEC) launched an investigation, which uncovered the full extent of the fraud.
- Thousands of employees lost their jobs, and investors lost billions of dollars.
- Several executives were indicted and convicted, including CEO Bernard Ebbers.
- The accounting firm Arthur Andersen, which audited WorldCom's books, was also implicated in the fraud and dissolved.
- The scandal led to calls for greater transparency and accountability in corporate governance and accounting practices.
- The Sarbanes-Oxley Act was passed to introduce stricter regulations for public

companies and their auditors to prevent accounting fraud.

T H R E E

Tyco International

Tyco International was a multinational corporation that provided various products and services ranging from security systems to medical devices. The company grew rapidly through a series of acquisitions in the 1990s and early 2000s, and at its peak, it had a market value of over $100 billion. However, in 2002, Tyco was exposed for engaging in massive accounting fraud, which resulted in the company's bankruptcy.

The fraud at Tyco was perpetrated by senior executives, including CEO Dennis Kozlowski and CFO Mark Swartz, who engaged in a range of illegal and unethical practices to enrich themselves at the company's expense. These practices included stealing company funds, inflating earnings, and engaging in insider trading.

One of the most significant aspects of the fraud was the misuse of company funds by Kozlowski and Swartz. They used company money to fund extravagant lifestyles, including purchases of luxury homes, yachts, and artwork. They also authorized large bonuses and compensation packages for themselves and other executives, which were not disclosed to shareholders.

Another key aspect of the fraud was the manipulation of the company's financial statements. Kozlowski and Swartz engaged in various accounting tricks to inflate Tyco's earnings and hide its expenses. They created fake invoices, shifted revenue between subsidiaries, and improperly accounted for stock options.

The fraud at Tyco was eventually uncovered by the Securities and Exchange Commission (SEC) and the New York Attorney General's office, which launched investigations into the company's accounting practices. Kozlowski and Swartz were indicted on charges of grand larceny, securities fraud, and other crimes. They were both convicted and sentenced to prison.

The fallout from the Tyco scandal was significant. The company's stock price plummeted, and it was forced to pay millions of dollars in fines and settlements to shareholders and regulators. The scandal also had broader implications for the corporate governance and accounting practices of large corporations.

In response to the Tyco scandal, the Sarbanes-Oxley Act was passed in 2002, which introduced stricter regulations for public companies and their auditors to prevent accounting fraud. The scandal also led to increased scrutiny of executive compensation and corporate governance practices.

Specifics of Tyco International fraud:

- Senior executives, including CEO Dennis Kozlowski and CFO Mark Swartz, engaged in a range of illegal and unethical practices to enrich themselves at the company's expense.
- The executives misused company funds to fund extravagant lifestyles, including purchases of luxury homes, yachts, and artwork.
- The executives authorized large bonuses and compensation packages for themselves and other executives, which were not disclosed to shareholders.
- The executives engaged in various accounting tricks to inflate Tyco's earnings and hide its expenses, including creating fake invoices, shifting revenue between subsidiaries, and improperly accounting for stock options.
- The fraud was uncovered by the Securities and Exchange Commission (SEC) and the New York Attorney General's office, which

launched investigations into the company's accounting practices.

- Kozlowski and Swartz were indicted on charges of grand larceny, securities fraud, and other crimes, and were both convicted and sentenced to prison.
- The scandal resulted in significant financial losses for shareholders and led to increased scrutiny of executive compensation and corporate governance practices.
- The Sarbanes-Oxley Act was passed in 2002 to introduce stricter regulations for public companies and their auditors to prevent accounting fraud.

FOUR

Bernie "Bernard' Madoff

Bernard "Bernie" Madoff was a financier and former chairman of the NASDAQ stock exchange. In 2008, Madoff was exposed for operating a massive Ponzi scheme that defrauded thousands of investors out of billions of dollars. The fraud was one of the largest and most significant in financial history and had far-reaching implications for the investment industry and regulatory agencies.

Madoff's Ponzi scheme operated for over 20 years, during which time he collected billions of dollars from investors under the guise of a legitimate investment advisory business. However, instead of investing the money, Madoff simply used new investor funds to pay out returns to earlier investors, while siphoning off millions of dollars for his own personal use.

The fraud at Madoff's investment firm, Bernard L. Madoff Investment Securities LLC, was facilitated by a number of factors, including a lack of regulatory oversight, a lack of transparency, and the willingness of investors to accept high returns without asking too many questions. Madoff was also able to use his reputation and connections within the financial industry to perpetrate fraud.

The scheme was eventually exposed in December 2008, when Madoff's sons contacted the authorities and revealed that their father had confessed to them that the investment advisory business was a fraud. The revelation triggered a massive investigation, and Madoff was arrested and charged with various crimes, including securities fraud, mail fraud, wire fraud, and money laundering.

The fallout from the Madoff scandal was significant. Thousands of investors lost their life savings, and many charitable organizations and non-profits were also affected. The scandal also had broader implications for the investment industry, as it highlighted the need for greater regulatory oversight and transparency.

In response to the Madoff scandal, the Securities and Exchange Commission (SEC) introduced a number of reforms, including new rules governing investment advisers, hedge funds, and other private funds. The scandal also led to increased scrutiny of the role of auditors and accounting firms in detecting and preventing financial fraud.

Specifics of Bernie Madoff fraud:

- Madoff operated a Ponzi scheme that defrauded thousands of investors out of billions of dollars over a period of more than 20 years.
- Madoff used new investor funds to pay out returns to earlier investors while siphoning off millions of dollars for his own personal use.
- The fraud was facilitated by a lack of regulatory oversight, a lack of transparency, and the willingness of investors to accept high returns without asking too many questions.
- Madoff's reputation and connections within the financial industry helped to perpetrate the fraud.
- Madoff was arrested and charged with various crimes, including securities fraud, mail fraud, wire fraud, and money laundering.
- The fallout from the Madoff scandal was significant, with thousands of investors losing their life savings and many charitable organizations and non-profits being affected.
- The scandal had broader implications for the investment industry, highlighting the need

for greater regulatory oversight and transparency.

- The Securities and Exchange Commission (SEC) introduced a number of reforms in response to the Madoff scandal, including new rules governing investment advisers, hedge funds, and other private funds.

F I V E

HealthSouth

HealthSouth was a US-based healthcare services company that became embroiled in one of the largest accounting scandals in American history. The scandal broke in 2003, when the company's founder and CEO, Richard Scrushy, was accused of orchestrating a massive fraud scheme that involved inflating the company's earnings by over $2.7 billion.

The fraud at HealthSouth was complex and involved a number of different techniques, including manipulating financial statements, inflating revenues, and hiding expenses. Scrushy was able to manipulate the company's financial results by pressuring senior executives to inflate earnings and by encouraging employees to conceal losses and write off expenses.

The scheme was uncovered by a whistleblower, who alerted the Securities and Exchange Commission (SEC) to irregularities in the company's accounting practices. The SEC launched an investigation, which eventually led to Scrushy being charged with 36 counts of accounting fraud, bribery, and obstruction of justice.

Scrushy's trial was highly publicized and lasted for several months. The prosecution presented evidence that Scrushy had engaged in a wide range of fraudulent activities, including creating fake invoices, falsifying bank statements, and manipulating the company's accounting records. The defense argued that Scrushy was unaware of the fraud and that he had been misled by his subordinates.

In the end, Scrushy was found not guilty on all counts, although he was later convicted of a separate bribery charge. However, a number of other senior executives at HealthSouth were convicted of fraud and sentenced to prison terms. The scandal had a significant impact on the company, which was forced to restate its earnings and pay a $325 million fine to settle SEC charges.

The fallout from the HealthSouth scandal was significant. It highlighted the need for greater regulatory oversight of the healthcare industry and led to a number of reforms in the areas of corporate governance and accounting practices. The scandal also had a significant impact on the reputation of the accounting firm Ernst & Young, which had audited HealthSouth's financial statements.

Specifics of HealthSouth Fraud:

- HealthSouth was a US-based healthcare services company that became embroiled in one of the largest accounting scandals in American history.
- The company's founder and CEO, Richard Scrushy, was accused of orchestrating a massive fraud scheme that involved inflating the company's earnings by over $2.7 billion.
- The fraud involved a number of techniques, including manipulating financial statements, inflating revenues, and hiding expenses.
- Scrushy was able to manipulate the company's financial results by pressuring senior executives to inflate earnings and by encouraging employees to conceal losses and write off expenses.
- The scheme was uncovered by a whistleblower, who alerted the Securities and Exchange Commission (SEC) to irregularities in the company's accounting practices.
- Scrushy was charged with 36 counts of accounting fraud, bribery, and obstruction of justice, but was ultimately found not guilty on all counts.

- A number of other senior executives at HealthSouth were convicted of fraud and sentenced to prison terms.
- The scandal had a significant impact on the company, which was forced to restate its earnings and pay a $325 million fine to settle SEC charges.
- The fallout from the HealthSouth scandal highlighted the need for greater regulatory oversight of the healthcare industry and led to a number of reforms in the areas of corporate governance and accounting practices.

SIX

Adelphia Communications

Adelphia Communications Corporation was a cable television company that was founded in 1952 by John Rigas and his family. It grew to become the fifth-largest cable company in the United States, with operations in over 30 states. However, in 2002, the company became embroiled in one of the largest corporate frauds in American history.

The fraud at Adelphia involved the Rigas family's mismanagement of the company's finances and the embezzlement of millions of dollars in funds. The family had used Adelphia as a personal piggy bank, siphoning off company funds for their own personal use, including the purchase of luxury homes and private jets.

The scheme was uncovered by the Securities and Exchange Commission (SEC) in March 2002, when the agency began investigating Adelphia's accounting practices. It was soon discovered that the company had overstated its earnings by more than $2 billion and that the Rigas family had hidden more than $2.3 billion in debt.

John Rigas and his sons, Timothy and Michael, were charged with multiple counts of securities fraud, wire fraud, and bank fraud. They were accused of inflating the company's earnings, lying about its financial condition, and using company funds for personal use. The Rigases were also accused of lying to investors and regulators about the company's finances.

In July 2002, Adelphia filed for bankruptcy protection, and the Rigases were forced to step down from their positions in the company. The SEC began an investigation, and the Rigases were eventually convicted of securities fraud, conspiracy, and other charges. John Rigas was sentenced to 15 years in prison, while Timothy and Michael were sentenced to 20 years each.

The fallout from the Adelphia fraud was significant. The company's bankruptcy had a ripple effect throughout the cable television industry, and many of its employees lost their jobs. The scandal also led to increased scrutiny of corporate accounting practices and a renewed focus on corporate governance and transparency.

Specifics of Adelphia Communications Fraud:

- Adelphia Communications Corporation was a cable television company that was founded in 1952 by John Rigas and his family.
- The company became embroiled in one of the largest corporate frauds in American history in 2002.
- The fraud involved the Rigas family's mismanagement of the company's finances and the embezzlement of millions of dollars in funds.
- The family had used Adelphia as a personal piggy bank, siphoning off company funds for their own personal use, including the purchase of luxury homes and private jets.
- The scheme was uncovered by the Securities and Exchange Commission (SEC) in March 2002, when the agency began investigating Adelphia's accounting practices.
- It was discovered that the company had overstated its earnings by more than $2 billion and that the Rigas family had hidden more than $2.3 billion in debt.
- John Rigas and his sons, Timothy and Michael, were charged with multiple counts

of securities fraud, wire fraud, and bank fraud.

- They were accused of inflating the company's earnings, lying about its financial condition, and using company funds for personal use.
- The Rigases were also accused of lying to investors and regulators about the company's finances.
- In July 2002, Adelphia filed for bankruptcy protection, and the Rigases were forced to step down from their positions in the company.
- The SEC began an investigation, and the Rigases were eventually convicted of securities fraud, conspiracy, and other charges.
- John Rigas was sentenced to 15 years in prison, while Timothy and Michael were sentenced to 20 years each.

SEVEN

Satyam Computer Services

Satyam Computer Services was a major Indian IT services company founded by B. Ramalinga Raju in 1987. The company was listed on the New York Stock Exchange (NYSE) and was one of the largest IT companies in India, providing services to major corporations worldwide. However, in 2009, the company became embroiled in one of the biggest corporate frauds in Indian history.

The fraud at Satyam involved Raju and other top executives inflating the company's earnings and assets by creating fake invoices and accounting entries. The company's auditors failed to detect the fraud, which had been going on for years.

The scandal came to light in January 2009, when Raju confessed to the fraud in a letter to the company's board of directors. In the letter, he admitted to inflating the company's earnings by over $1 billion and stated that the company's cash balances were also inflated.

Following the confession, the Indian government stepped in and took control of the company, appointing a new board of directors. The company's auditors, PriceWaterhouseCoopers (PWC), were also investigated for their role in the fraud.

The fallout from the Satyam scandal was significant, with the company's share price falling by over 80% and many clients terminating their contracts with the company. Raju and other top executives were arrested and charged with fraud, forgery, and criminal conspiracy.

In 2015, Raju and the other accused were found guilty and sentenced to imprisonment. Raju was sentenced to seven years in prison, while the other accused received varying sentences.

The Satyam scandal had a profound impact on the Indian IT industry, leading to increased scrutiny of corporate governance and accounting practices. It also highlighted the need for stronger regulations and oversight to prevent similar frauds in the future.

Specifics of Satyam Computer Services Fraud:

- Satyam Computer Services was a major Indian IT services company founded by B. Ramalinga Raju in 1987.

- The company became embroiled in one of the biggest corporate frauds in Indian history in 2009.
- The fraud involved Raju and other top executives inflating the company's earnings and assets by creating fake invoices and accounting entries.
- The company's auditors failed to detect the fraud, which had been going on for years.
- The scandal came to light in January 2009, when Raju confessed to the fraud in a letter to the company's board of directors.
- In the letter, he admitted to inflating the company's earnings by over $1 billion and stated that the company's cash balances were also inflated.
- Following the confession, the Indian government stepped in and took control of the company, appointing a new board of directors.
- The company's auditors, PriceWaterhouseCoopers, were also investigated for their role in the fraud.
- Raju and other top executives were arrested and charged with fraud, forgery, and criminal conspiracy.
- The fallout from the Satyam scandal was significant, with the company's share price

falling by over 80% and many clients terminating their contracts with the company.

- In 2015, Raju and the other accused were found guilty and sentenced to imprisonment.
- The Satyam scandal had a profound impact on the Indian IT industry, leading to increased scrutiny of corporate governance and accounting practices.
- It also highlighted the need for stronger regulations and oversight to prevent similar frauds in the future.

EIGHT

Parmalat

Parmalat was a multinational Italian dairy and food corporation that was founded in 1961. It was one of the largest food companies in the world, with operations in more than 30 countries. However, in 2003, the company became embroiled in one of the biggest corporate frauds in European history.

The fraud at Parmalat involved the company's founder and CEO, Calisto Tanzi, and other top executives creating a complex network of offshore companies and bank accounts to hide the company's true financial position. They used these offshore entities to make false transactions and inflate the company's assets and earnings.

The fraud was initially discovered in December 2003 when Parmalat was unable to make a bond payment of €150 million. It was subsequently revealed that the company had been overstating its assets by over €14 billion.

Following the discovery of the fraud, Parmalat declared bankruptcy, and thousands of investors lost their money. The Italian government launched an investigation into the fraud, which resulted in criminal charges being brought against Tanzi and other top executives.

Tanzi was arrested and charged with fraud and embezzlement, and in 2008, he was sentenced to ten years in prison. Other executives were also arrested and charged, with some receiving lengthy prison sentences.

The Parmalat scandal had a significant impact on the Italian economy and highlighted the need for stronger regulation and oversight of corporate governance and accounting practices.

Specifics of Parmalat Fraud:

- Parmalat was a multinational Italian dairy and food corporation founded in 1961.
- In 2003, the company became embroiled in one of the biggest corporate frauds in European history.
- The fraud involved the company's founder and CEO, Calisto Tanzi, and other top executives creating a complex network of

- offshore companies and bank accounts to hide the company's true financial position.
- They used these offshore entities to make false transactions and inflate the company's assets and earnings.
- The fraud was discovered in December 2003 when Parmalat was unable to make a bond payment of €150 million.
- It was subsequently revealed that the company had been overstating its assets by over €14 billion.
- Following the discovery of the fraud, Parmalat declared bankruptcy, and thousands of investors lost their money.
- The Italian government launched an investigation into the fraud, which resulted in criminal charges being brought against Tanzi and other top executives.
- Tanzi was arrested and charged with fraud and embezzlement, and in 2008, he was sentenced to ten years in prison.
- Other executives were also arrested and charged, with some receiving lengthy prison sentences.
- The Parmalat scandal had a significant impact on the Italian economy and highlighted the need for stronger regulation

and oversight of corporate governance and accounting practices.

NINE

AIG

American International Group (AIG) was one of the world's largest insurance companies, with operations in more than 130 countries. It was founded in 1919 and became a major player in the insurance industry. However, in 2008, the company became embroiled in a scandal that threatened its very existence.

The AIG scandal involved the company's Financial Products unit, which had sold credit default swaps (CDSs) to banks and other investors. CDSs are a type of insurance policy that protects investors against default on a particular bond or other financial instrument.

The Financial Products unit had sold billions of dollars worth of CDSs, but it had not set aside enough money to cover potential losses. When the housing market crashed and defaults on subprime mortgages began to soar, AIG was left on the hook for billions of dollars in payouts.

The company was unable to cover these losses, and in September 2008, it was forced to seek a government bailout of $85 billion. This was the largest government bailout in history at the time.

The AIG scandal also revealed other questionable practices at the company, including accounting irregularities and insider trading. The company had been using an offshore entity called AIG Financial Products Corp. to move assets and liabilities off its balance sheet, making it appear more financially sound than it actually was.

In addition, several top executives at the company were found to have engaged in insider trading, including the CEO, Hank Greenberg. Greenberg was forced to resign in 2005, but he continued to deny any wrongdoing.

The AIG scandal had a significant impact on the US economy, and it led to increased scrutiny of the financial industry and calls for stronger regulation.

Specifics of AIG Fraud:

- American International Group (AIG) was one of the world's largest insurance companies.
- The AIG scandal involved the company's Financial Products unit, which had sold

credit default swaps (CDSs) to banks and other investors.

- The Financial Products unit had sold billions of dollars worth of CDSs, but it had not set aside enough money to cover potential losses.
- When the housing market crashed and defaults on subprime mortgages began to soar, AIG was left on the hook for billions of dollars in payouts.
- The company was unable to cover these losses, and in September 2008, it was forced to seek a government bailout of $85 billion.
- The AIG scandal also revealed other questionable practices at the company, including accounting irregularities and insider trading.
- The company had been using an offshore entity called AIG Financial Products Corp. to move assets and liabilities off its balance sheet, making it appear more financially sound than it actually was.
- Several top executives at the company were found to have engaged in insider trading, including the CEO, Hank Greenberg.
- Greenberg was forced to resign in 2005, but he continued to deny any wrongdoing.

- The AIG scandal had a significant impact on the US economy, and it led to increased scrutiny of the financial industry and calls for stronger regulation.

TEN

Olympus

Olympus Corporation, a Japanese company founded in 1919, is a leading manufacturer of optical and imaging equipment, including cameras, microscopes, and medical devices. However, in 2011, the company was embroiled in a scandal involving accounting fraud and cover-ups that shook the business world.

The Olympus scandal began to unfold in October 2011 when the company's then-CEO, Michael Woodford, was abruptly fired after he raised concerns about questionable payments made by the company. Woodford had only been in the role for a few weeks, having been promoted from his previous position as head of Olympus's European operations.

Woodford had become suspicious after he discovered a series of payments worth $687 million that had been made to obscure advisory firms in the Cayman Islands and elsewhere. Woodford believed that these payments were suspicious and that they might be covering up losses incurred by the company's previous investments.

After raising his concerns with the company's board, Woodford was fired. However, he refused to go quietly and instead went public with his allegations, accusing the company of a cover-up and fraud. He also shared documents and recordings with the media, which appeared to support his claims.

As the scandal unfolded, it emerged that Olympus had been using a complex system of accounting tricks to hide its losses. The company had been inflating the value of its assets for years by using acquisitions and goodwill write-offs. These accounting irregularities had gone unnoticed for years and had allowed the company to hide its losses.

Olympus was also found to have paid huge sums of money to investment banks and financial advisors, who had helped to cover up the losses. The company had also set up fake companies in order to make it appear that the payments were legitimate.

In the wake of the scandal, Olympus was forced to restate its financial statements, which revealed that it had been overstating its assets by $1.7 billion. The company's shares plummeted, and it faced the possibility of delisting from the Tokyo Stock Exchange.

Several executives at Olympus were later arrested and charged with fraud, including the company's former chairman, Tsuyoshi Kikukawa. The company eventually reached a settlement with the US Securities and Exchange Commission (SEC) and paid a $92 million fine to the US government.

The Olympus scandal was a major blow to the reputation of Japanese corporate governance and led to increased scrutiny of the country's business practices. It also highlighted the importance of whistleblowers in uncovering fraud and corruption.

Specifics of Olympus Fraud:

- The Olympus scandal involved accounting fraud and cover-ups that shook the business world.
- The scandal began to unfold in October 2011 when the company's then-CEO, Michael Woodford, was abruptly fired after he raised concerns about questionable payments made by the company.
- Woodford became suspicious after he discovered a series of payments worth $687 million that had been made to obscure

advisory firms in the Cayman Islands and elsewhere.

- It emerged that Olympus had been using a complex system of accounting tricks to hide its losses, including inflating the value of its assets for years by using acquisitions and goodwill write-offs.
- Olympus was also found to have paid huge sums of money to investment banks and financial advisors, who had helped to cover up the losses.
- The company had set up fake companies in order to make it appear that the payments were legitimate.
- In the wake of the scandal, Olympus was forced to restate its financial statements, which revealed that it had been overstating its assets by $1.7 billion.
- Several executives at Olympus were later arrested and charged with fraud, including the company's former chairman, Tsuyoshi Kikukawa.
- The company eventually reached a settlement with the US Securities and Exchange Commission (SEC) and paid a $92 million fine.

ELEVEN

Volkswagen

Volkswagen, the German car manufacturer, was embroiled in a major scandal in 2015 when it was revealed that the company had been cheating on emissions tests for its diesel vehicles. The scandal rocked the automotive industry and led to widespread public outrage.

The fraud was discovered by the US Environmental Protection Agency (EPA) in September 2015, which found that Volkswagen had installed software in its diesel vehicles that could detect when the cars were being tested for emissions and reduce the levels of harmful pollutants accordingly. However, when the cars were on the road, the emissions levels were much higher than the legal limit.

The software, known as a "defeat device," allowed Volkswagen to pass emissions tests and market its diesel vehicles as environmentally friendly, while in reality, they were emitting up to 40 times more nitrogen oxide than allowed by US law. This deception affected around 11 million diesel vehicles worldwide.

The revelation of the fraud led to a significant drop in Volkswagen's stock price, with the company losing around a third of its market value in the days following the announcement. The scandal also led to the resignation of Volkswagen's CEO, Martin Winterkorn, and a number of other senior executives.

The fallout from the scandal has been extensive, with the company paying out billions of dollars in fines and compensation to customers and regulators. In 2017, Volkswagen pleaded guilty to criminal charges in the United States and agreed to pay a $2.8 billion fine. The company also agreed to pay $14.7 billion in a settlement with US regulators and vehicle owners.

The Volkswagen scandal has had far-reaching consequences, both for the company and the wider automotive industry. It has led to increased scrutiny of emissions testing and has prompted calls for more stringent regulations. The scandal has also highlighted the importance of ethical business practices and the need for transparency and accountability.

Specifics of Volkswagen Fraud:

- Volkswagen installed software in its diesel vehicles that could detect when the cars were being tested for emissions and reduce the levels of harmful pollutants accordingly.
- The software allowed Volkswagen to pass emissions tests and market its diesel vehicles as environmentally friendly, while in reality, they were emitting up to 40 times more nitrogen oxide than allowed by US law.
- The deception affected around 11 million diesel vehicles worldwide.
- The scandal led to a significant drop in Volkswagen's stock price, with the company losing around a third of its market value in the days following the announcement.
- The scandal led to the resignation of Volkswagen's CEO, Martin Winterkorn, and a number of other senior executives.
- The company has paid out billions of dollars in fines and compensation to customers and regulators.
- In 2017, Volkswagen pleaded guilty to criminal charges in the United States and agreed to pay a $2.8 billion fine.

- The company also agreed to pay $14.7 billion in a settlement with US regulators and vehicle owners.
- The scandal has led to increased scrutiny of emissions testing and has prompted calls for more stringent regulations.
- The scandal has highlighted the importance of ethical business practices and the need for transparency and accountability in the automotive industry.

TWELVE

Wells Fargo

Wells Fargo, one of the largest banks in the United States, was involved in a major scandal in 2016 when it was revealed that the company had opened millions of unauthorized bank accounts for its customers. The scandal resulted in the firing of thousands of employees, a significant drop in the bank's stock price, and a $185 million settlement with US regulators.

The fraud was discovered by the Consumer Financial Protection Bureau (CFPB), which found that Wells Fargo employees had opened more than two million bank accounts and credit card accounts for customers without their knowledge or consent. The employees had used customers' personal information to open the accounts, often without their knowledge, in order to meet aggressive sales targets and earn bonuses.

The scandal was initially uncovered by an investigation by the Los Angeles Times, which revealed that employees at Wells Fargo had been engaging in fraudulent activity for years. The bank had fired around 5,300 employees in connection with the scandal, but critics argued that the company had not done enough to address the issue or compensate affected customers.

In response to the scandal, Wells Fargo's CEO, John Stumpf, was forced to resign, and the company launched an internal review of its sales practices. The bank also agreed to pay a $185 million settlement with US regulators, which was the largest ever paid by a bank for such conduct.

The scandal had far-reaching consequences, with the bank's stock price dropping significantly in the days following the announcement. The scandal also led to increased scrutiny of the banking industry and prompted calls for greater regulation and oversight.

Specifics of Wells Fargo Fraud:

- Wells Fargo employees opened more than two million bank accounts and credit card accounts for customers without their knowledge or consent.
- The employees used customers' personal information to open the accounts, often

without their knowledge, in order to meet aggressive sales targets and earn bonuses.

- The scandal was initially uncovered by an investigation by the Los Angeles Times, which revealed that employees at Wells Fargo had been engaging in fraudulent activity for years.
- The bank had fired around 5,300 employees in connection with the scandal.
- The scandal led to the resignation of Wells Fargo's CEO, John Stumpf.
- The bank agreed to pay a $185 million settlement with US regulators, which was the largest ever paid by a bank for such conduct.
- The scandal had far-reaching consequences, with the bank's stock price dropping significantly in the days following the announcement.
- The scandal led to increased scrutiny of the banking industry and prompted calls for greater regulation and oversight.
- The scandal highlighted the importance of ethical business practices and the need for transparency and accountability in the banking industry.

THIRTEEN

Petrobras

Petrobras, a Brazilian state-owned oil company, was involved in one of the largest corruption scandals in the country's history, known as the "Operation Car Wash" scandal. The scandal, which was first uncovered in 2014, involved a massive corruption scheme that had been operating within Petrobras for years and implicated some of the country's most powerful politicians and businesspeople.

The scheme involved a complex web of bribes and kickbacks paid to Petrobras executives and politicians in exchange for lucrative contracts with the company. The bribes were paid by construction companies in Brazil, which formed a cartel that rigged contracts with Petrobras to inflate the prices of their services. The bribes were then funneled back to Petrobras executives and politicians, who used the money to enrich themselves and their political parties.

The scandal was first uncovered by Brazilian investigators, who launched an extensive investigation known as "Operation Car Wash." The investigation led to the arrest of dozens of executives and politicians, including several high-ranking officials at Petrobras.

As the scandal unfolded, it became clear that the corruption had been deeply entrenched within Petrobras for years. The company had been operating a "culture of corruption," in which bribes and kickbacks were seen as a routine part of doing business. The scandal ultimately resulted in the loss of billions of dollars for Petrobras and significant damage to Brazil's economy and political system.

The scandal also had far-reaching consequences for the oil industry and global markets. Petrobras, which had been one of the world's most valuable companies, saw its stock price plummet, and the scandal sparked concerns about corruption and instability in emerging markets.

In response to the scandal, Petrobras launched an internal investigation and implemented new measures to improve transparency and accountability. The company also agreed to pay billions of dollars in fines and settlements to Brazilian and US authorities.

Specifics of Petrobras Fraud:

- The Petrobras fraud involved a massive corruption scheme that had been operating within the company for years.
- The scheme involved a complex web of bribes and kickbacks paid to Petrobras executives and politicians in exchange for lucrative contracts with the company.
- The bribes were paid by construction companies in Brazil, which formed a cartel that rigged contracts with Petrobras to inflate the prices of their services.
- The bribes were then funneled back to Petrobras executives and politicians, who used the money to enrich themselves and their political parties.
- The scandal was first uncovered by Brazilian investigators, who launched an extensive investigation known as "Operation Car Wash."
- The investigation led to the arrest of dozens of executives and politicians, including several high-ranking officials at Petrobras.
- The scandal revealed that corruption had been deeply entrenched within Petrobras for years, and the company had been operating a "culture of corruption."

- The scandal resulted in the loss of billions of dollars for Petrobras and significant damage to Brazil's economy and political system.
- The scandal had far-reaching consequences for the oil industry and global markets, and sparked concerns about corruption and instability in emerging markets.
- Petrobras launched an internal investigation and implemented new measures to improve transparency and accountability.
- The company agreed to pay billions of dollars in fines and settlements to Brazilian and US authorities.

In conclusion, the Petrobras fraud was one of the largest corruption scandals in Brazil's history and had significant consequences for the country's economy and political system. The scandal revealed the extent of corruption within Petrobras and underscored the importance of transparency and accountability in business and government. While the scandal had far-reaching consequences, it also served as a wake-up call for Brazil and other emerging markets, highlighting the need for stronger regulations and greater oversight to prevent similar abuses in the future.

FOURTEEN

Toshiba

Toshiba is a Japanese multinational conglomerate that produces a wide range of products, including consumer electronics, semiconductors, and infrastructure services. The company has a long and storied history dating back to its founding in 1875. However, in recent years, Toshiba has been embroiled in a scandal involving accounting fraud, which has severely damaged its reputation and financial position.

The Toshiba scandal began to emerge in 2015 when the company revealed that it had overstated its profits by $1.2 billion over the course of seven years. The revelation was shocking and rocked the company, as it had been seen as a pillar of Japanese corporate governance and excellence.

Accounting fraud was carried out in a number of ways. For example, the company's executives pressured subordinates to meet unrealistic profit targets, which led to accounting irregularities. Additionally, Toshiba's accounting department manipulated its financial statements by using accounting techniques that were illegal or at the very least, questionable.

As the scandal unfolded, a number of top executives were forced to resign, including then-CEO Hisao Tanaka. In addition, the company was fined by regulators in Japan, and its reputation was severely damaged. The scandal also led to a major shake-up in Japanese corporate governance, as many questioned the effectiveness of the country's regulatory framework.

One of the key factors in the Toshiba scandal was the company's corporate culture, which placed a high premium on conformity and loyalty to the company. This culture made it difficult for employees to speak out against wrongdoing or to challenge senior executives. In addition, there were concerns about the effectiveness of Toshiba's internal controls and auditing procedures, which failed to detect the accounting irregularities.

In response to the scandal, Toshiba undertook a number of measures to improve its corporate governance and financial reporting. For example, the company appointed an independent committee to investigate accounting fraud and recommend changes to the company's governance structure. In addition, Toshiba has implemented a number of measures to improve transparency and accountability, such as strengthening its internal controls and increasing the independence of its board of directors.

The fallout from the Toshiba scandal has been significant. The company's reputation has been severely damaged, and it has struggled to regain the trust of investors and customers. In addition, the company's financial position has been weakened, as it has had to pay significant fines and settlements related to the scandal.

Specifics of the fraud:

- In July 2015, Toshiba announced that it had overstated its profits by $1.2 billion over the course of seven years.
- The accounting fraud was carried out in a number of ways, including pressure on subordinates to meet unrealistic profit targets and manipulation of financial statements.
- As a result of the scandal, then-CEO Hisao Tanaka and a number of other top executives were forced to resign.
- Toshiba was fined by regulators in Japan, and its reputation was severely damaged.

- The scandal led to a major shake-up in Japanese corporate governance, as many questioned the effectiveness of the country's regulatory framework.
- Toshiba appointed an independent committee to investigate the accounting fraud and recommend changes to the company's governance structure.
- Toshiba has implemented measures to improve transparency and accountability, such as strengthening its internal controls and increasing the independence of its board of directors.
- The fallout from the scandal has been significant, with Toshiba's reputation severely damaged and its financial position weakened.

FIFTEEN

Barclays

Barclays is a British multinational investment bank and financial services company. In 2012, the bank became embroiled in a major scandal involving fraudulent behavior by its traders and the manipulation of interest rates. The scandal resulted in significant fines for the bank and a loss of public trust in the institution.

The Barclays fraud scandal involved the manipulation of the London Interbank Offered Rate (LIBOR) and the Euro Interbank Offered Rate (Euribor). These are the interest rates that banks use to lend to one another, and they are used as benchmarks for a wide range of financial instruments, including mortgages and loans.

The manipulation of these interest rates by Barclays traders was carried out in a number of ways. For example, traders would submit false information to the panel of banks responsible for setting the LIBOR and Euribor rates. They would also make false trades in order to influence the rates in their favor.

The manipulation of these rates had a significant impact on the financial markets. For example, if the LIBOR rate was artificially lowered, it would make it cheaper for banks to borrow money from one another. This could result in lower interest rates for customers, which would have a positive impact on the economy. However, if the rates were artificially raised, it would have the opposite effect, making it more expensive for banks to borrow money and potentially leading to higher interest rates for customers.

The Barclays fraud scandal was first uncovered in 2012 when regulators in the US and UK began investigating the manipulation of LIBOR and Euribor rates. The investigation revealed that Barclays traders had manipulated the rates over a period of several years, from 2005 to 2009. The bank was fined £290 million ($453 million) by regulators in the UK and the US as a result of the scandal.

In addition to the fines, the scandal also had significant consequences for the bank's reputation. The CEO at the time, Bob Diamond, was forced to resign, and the bank faced a public backlash. The scandal also led to a wider investigation into the manipulation of interest rates by other banks, which resulted in fines for a number of other financial institutions.

Following the scandal, Barclays has implemented a number of measures to improve its governance and risk management practices. The bank has also introduced a whistleblower program to encourage employees to report any wrongdoing they observe. In addition, the bank has increased its regulatory compliance team and strengthened its internal controls.

Specifics of the fraud:

- The Barclays fraud scandal involved the manipulation of the London Interbank Offered Rate (LIBOR) and the Euro Interbank Offered Rate (Euribor).
- The manipulation of these rates was carried out by Barclays traders submitting false information and making false trades to influence the rates in their favor.
- The scandal was first uncovered in 2012 and resulted in fines of £290 million ($453 million) for the bank.
- The scandal had significant consequences for the bank's reputation, with the CEO at the time, Bob Diamond, forced to resign and the bank facing a public backlash.

- Following the scandal, Barclays implemented measures to improve its governance and risk management practices, including a whistleblower program, increased regulatory compliance team, and strengthened internal controls.

SIXTEEN

The Royal Bank of Scotland

The Royal Bank of Scotland (RBS) is a Scottish multinational banking and financial services company headquartered in Edinburgh. In 2010, the bank became embroiled in a major scandal involving the mis-selling of complex financial products to small businesses. The scandal resulted in significant fines for the bank and a loss of public trust in the institution.

The RBS fraud scandal involved the sale of complex financial products known as interest rate swaps to small businesses. These products were designed to help businesses manage their interest rate risk but were often unsuitable for the businesses that were sold them. As a result, many businesses suffered significant financial losses when interest rates moved in unexpected ways.

The mis-selling of these products was carried out by RBS staff who often lacked the necessary training and expertise to understand the risks involved. In addition, there was evidence that staff were incentivized to sell these products, even when they were not suitable for the businesses they were being sold to.

The RBS fraud scandal was first uncovered in 2010 when small businesses began to report significant losses as a result of the interest rate swaps they had been sold. An investigation by the UK Financial Services Authority (FSA) found that RBS had engaged in "serious failings" in the sale of these products and that many of the businesses affected had been treated unfairly.

As a result of the scandal, RBS was fined £390 million ($525 million) by regulators in the UK and the US. The bank also set aside a further £400 million ($538 million) to compensate businesses affected by the mis-selling of these products.

The scandal had significant consequences for the bank's reputation, with a loss of public trust in the institution. It also led to a wider investigation into the mis-selling of financial products by other banks, which resulted in fines for a number of other financial institutions.

Following the scandal, RBS has implemented a number of measures to improve its governance and risk management practices. The bank has also introduced a compensation scheme for businesses affected by the mis-selling of interest rate swaps.

Specifics of the fraud:

- The RBS fraud scandal involved the mis-selling of complex financial products known as interest rate swaps to small businesses.
- The mis-selling was carried out by RBS staff who often lacked the necessary training and expertise to understand the risks involved, and who were incentivized to sell these products.
- The scandal was first uncovered in 2010 and resulted in fines of £390 million ($525 million) for the bank.
- The scandal had significant consequences for the bank's reputation, with a loss of public trust in the institution.
- Following the scandal, RBS implemented measures to improve its governance and risk management practices, including a compensation scheme for businesses affected by the mis-selling of interest rate swaps.

SEVENTEEN

Tesco

Tesco is a British multinational retailer that operates in the grocery and general merchandise market. In 2014, the company became embroiled in a major scandal involving accounting irregularities. The scandal resulted in significant fines for the company, a loss of public trust, and a period of significant financial difficulties.

The Tesco fraud scandal involved the manipulation of the company's financial statements in order to overstate profits. This was done by accelerating the recognition of income and delaying the recognition of expenses, in order to make the company's financial performance appear stronger than it actually was.

The fraud was carried out by a group of senior executives at the company, including the CFO and the head of UK operations. These individuals were motivated by a desire to meet profit targets and maintain the company's strong reputation with investors and analysts.

The fraud was first uncovered in September 2014, when an internal investigation by Tesco identified a discrepancy in its accounts. This led to the suspension of several executives, including the CFO, and an investigation by the UK's Serious Fraud Office (SFO).

In 2017, three former Tesco executives were charged with fraud and false accounting in relation to the scandal. The executives were accused of inflating Tesco's profits by £250 million ($336 million) over a period of three years.

In March 2018, the three executives were found guilty of fraud and false accounting. They were each sentenced to prison terms ranging from 18 months to three years. In addition, Tesco was fined £129 million ($173 million) by the UK's Financial Reporting Council (FRC) for "failing to exercise sufficient care and diligence" in relation to its accounts.

The Tesco fraud scandal had significant consequences for the company's reputation and financial performance. The company's share price fell sharply following the announcement of the scandal, and it experienced a period of significant financial difficulties.

Since the scandal, Tesco has implemented a number of measures to improve its governance and risk management practices. The company has appointed a new CEO and CFO, and has made significant changes to its accounting policies and procedures.

Specifics of the fraud:

- The Tesco fraud scandal involved the manipulation of the company's financial statements in order to overstate profits.
- The fraud was carried out by a group of senior executives at the company, who were motivated by a desire to meet profit targets and maintain the company's reputation.
- The fraud was first uncovered in 2014, leading to the suspension of several executives and an investigation by the UK's Serious Fraud Office.
- In 2017, three former Tesco executives were charged with fraud and false accounting in relation to the scandal.
- In 2018, the three executives were found guilty and sentenced to prison terms, and Tesco was fined £129 million ($173 million) by the UK's Financial Reporting Council.
- The scandal had significant consequences for the company's reputation and financial

performance, with a loss of public trust and a period of significant financial difficulties.

- Since the scandal, Tesco has implemented measures to improve its governance and risk management practices, including changes to its accounting policies and procedures.

EIGHTEEN
Kobe Steel

Kobe Steel Ltd. is a Japanese multinational corporation with its headquarters located in Kobe, Japan. The company was established in 1905 and has since grown into a major steel manufacturer with operations in Japan, Asia, Europe, and the Americas. In 2017, Kobe Steel was embroiled in a major fraud scandal, which shocked the global business community and led to significant damage to the company's reputation.

The Kobe Steel fraud scandal came to light in October 2017 when the company disclosed that it had falsified data related to the quality of its aluminum, copper, and steel products. The company had been falsely certifying the quality of its products for years, including products used in automobiles, airplanes, and even nuclear power plants. This revelation led to a recall of over 500 million products and severely impacted the company's financial performance.

Kobe Steel's fraudulent activities involved falsifying inspection data for its products to make them appear to meet customer specifications. The company would manipulate test results to meet the requested specifications even when the product did not meet those requirements. The fraud was facilitated by a lack of proper internal controls and oversight, as well as a culture of putting profits ahead of product quality and safety.

The Kobe Steel fraud scandal had significant implications for the company's reputation and financial performance. The company's stock price fell by nearly 40% within days of the scandal being revealed, and the company was forced to issue an apology to its customers and stakeholders. The scandal also led to significant regulatory and legal scrutiny, including investigations by the Japanese government and regulatory bodies in other countries.

As a result of the scandal, Kobe Steel was forced to take a number of steps to address the issue and restore its reputation. The company implemented a new corporate governance system, which included the appointment of independent directors to its board. It also established a new Quality Assurance Division to oversee the quality of its products and improve its internal controls and compliance practices.

Kobe Steel also faced significant legal and financial consequences as a result of the fraud scandal. The company was fined by regulatory bodies in Japan and the United States and faced a number of shareholder lawsuits. In addition, the company was forced to raise capital through a public offering to address the financial impact of the scandal.

Specifics of the Kobe Steel fraud:

- The fraud involved falsifying data related to the quality of aluminium, copper, and steel products.
- The company had been falsely certifying the quality of its products for years.
- The fraud impacted products used in automobiles, airplanes, and nuclear power plants.
- The fraud was facilitated by a lack of proper internal controls and oversight.
- The fraud was driven by a culture of putting profits ahead of product quality and safety.
- The company's stock price fell by nearly 40% within days of the scandal being revealed.
- The scandal led to a recall of over 500 million products.

- The scandal led to significant regulatory and legal scrutiny, including investigations by the Japanese government and regulatory bodies in other countries.
- Kobe Steel implemented a new corporate governance system following the scandal, which included the appointment of independent directors to its board.
- The company established a new Quality Assurance Division to oversee the quality of its products and improve its internal controls and compliance practices.
- Kobe Steel faced fines from regulatory bodies in Japan and the United States and several shareholder lawsuits as a result of the scandal.
- The company was forced to raise capital through a public offering to address the financial impact of the scandal.

In conclusion, the Kobe Steel fraud scandal was a significant event in the history of the company and the global business community. The scandal exposed weaknesses in the company's corporate governance, internal controls, and culture, and had severe consequences for its reputation and financial performance. The company has since taken steps to address these issues and restore its reputation, but the scandal remains a cautionary tale of the importance of proper corporate governance, internal controls, and compliance practices in today's global business environment.

NINETEEN

Steinhoff International

Steinhoff International is a South African multinational retail holding company that specializes in furniture and household goods. It was founded in 1964 and grew into one of the largest retailers in the world, with operations in over 30 countries and a portfolio of well-known brands such as Conforama, Mattress Firm, and Poundland. However, in 2017, Steinhoff was rocked by one of the biggest accounting scandals in corporate history, which led to significant financial losses and a sharp decline in its share price.

The Steinhoff scandal was first uncovered in December 2017, when the company announced that its CEO, Markus Jooste, had resigned and that it had launched an investigation into accounting irregularities. The investigation revealed that the company had engaged in fraudulent accounting practices, including inflating its revenue and profits and manipulating its financial statements. The fraud had been ongoing for several years and had gone undetected by auditors and regulators.

One of the key aspects of the fraud was the use of off-balance sheet vehicles to hide losses and debt. These vehicles were used to purchase assets that were later sold back to Steinhoff at inflated prices, allowing the company to artificially boost its revenue and profits. The fraud also involved the overstatement of inventory levels and the manipulation of foreign exchange rates.

The consequences of the Steinhoff scandal were significant. The company's share price collapsed, losing over 90% of its value in just a few days. Investors lost billions of dollars, and many were left wondering how such a massive fraud could have gone undetected for so long. The scandal also led to a loss of confidence in the South African economy and raised questions about the quality of corporate governance and oversight in the country.

The fallout from the scandal continues to this day. Steinhoff has faced numerous lawsuits from investors and creditors, and the company has been forced to sell off many of its assets to pay down debt. The company has also been subject to regulatory investigations in several countries, including South Africa, Germany, and the Netherlands.

In response to the scandal, Steinhoff has taken several steps to address the issues that led to the fraud. The company has appointed a new board of directors, including several independent directors, and has implemented a new corporate governance framework. The company has also taken steps to improve its financial reporting and accounting practices, including the appointment of new auditors and the establishment of a dedicated forensic investigation team.

Despite these efforts, the fallout from the Steinhoff scandal is likely to be felt for many years to come. The case highlights the importance of strong corporate governance and oversight, and the need for investors and regulators to be vigilant in detecting and preventing fraudulent accounting practices. It also raises questions about the role of auditors in detecting and reporting fraud and the need for greater accountability and transparency in the auditing profession.

Specifics of the Steinhoff International fraud:

- The fraud was discovered in late 2017 when the company's CEO, Markus Jooste, resigned abruptly and the company's share price plummeted.

- It was revealed that Steinhoff had engaged in accounting irregularities for several years, inflating its profits and assets.
- The fraud involved the creation of fictitious transactions and the manipulation of financial statements to hide the true state of the company's finances.
- Steinhoff's auditors, Deloitte, failed to uncover the fraud, leading to criticism of the auditing industry as a whole.
- The fraud affected numerous investors, including large institutional investors and small retail investors.
- The fallout from the fraud led to the collapse of Steinhoff's share price and caused significant losses for investors.
- Steinhoff's former CEO, Markus Jooste, was implicated in the fraud and has faced criminal charges.
- In addition to the fraud, Steinhoff was also accused of unethical business practices, including the mistreatment of suppliers and employees.
- The company has faced numerous lawsuits and regulatory investigations in the aftermath of the fraud.
- Steinhoff has been working to restructure its business and settle legal claims related to the

fraud, but the full extent of the financial damage caused by the fraud is still being assessed.

- The Steinhoff scandal has led to increased scrutiny of corporate governance and accounting practices in South Africa, where the company is based, and has highlighted the need for greater accountability and transparency in the corporate sector.

In summary, the Steinhoff scandal was one of the biggest accounting frauds in corporate history, and its impact was felt not only by the company and its investors but also by the wider business community and the South African economy. The scandal serves as a cautionary tale of the importance of strong corporate governance and oversight, and the need for greater transparency and accountability in financial reporting and auditing practices.

TWENTY

Wirecard

Wirecard was a German payments processing company that gained international attention after a massive accounting scandal was uncovered in June 2020. The scandal involved allegations of fraud, money laundering, and accounting irregularities, which ultimately led to the company filing for insolvency and criminal investigations being launched against its executives. In this article, we will discuss the events that led to the Wirecard scandal and the impact it had on the financial industry.

Background of Wirecard

Wirecard was founded in 1999 as a provider of electronic payment and risk management services. The company was based in Munich, Germany, and quickly grew to become one of the leading payments processors in Europe, serving clients in industries ranging from retail to travel and hospitality.

The company's growth was driven by a series of acquisitions and partnerships, which helped it expand its global reach and diversify its services. In 2018, Wirecard became the first German technology company to achieve a market valuation of over €20 billion, making it one of the most valuable companies in Europe.

The Wirecard Scandal

In early 2019, the Financial Times published a series of articles alleging that Wirecard had engaged in fraudulent accounting practices, including inflating its revenue and profits. The articles cited leaked documents and interviews with former employees, who claimed that the company had used a complex web of shell companies and fake transactions to fabricate its financial results.

Wirecard initially denied the allegations, but the reports triggered an investigation by the German financial regulator, BaFin, and the appointment of KPMG to conduct an independent audit of the company's accounts. The audit, which was completed in April 2020, found that Wirecard had failed to provide sufficient documentation for many of its transactions and raised serious concerns about the reliability of the company's financial reporting.

Despite the audit's findings, Wirecard continued to assert its innocence and tried to discredit the whistleblowers and journalists who had exposed the alleged fraud. The company's CEO, Markus Braun, also announced plans to launch a legal action against the Financial Times for defamation.

However, in June 2020, Wirecard admitted that €1.9 billion was missing from its accounts, and that the money may never have existed in the first place. The revelation sparked a crisis of confidence in the company, and its share price plummeted. Wirecard filed for insolvency just days later, and an investigation was launched by German authorities into allegations of fraud, embezzlement, and market manipulation.

The Impact of the Wirecard Scandal

The Wirecard scandal had far-reaching consequences for the financial industry, exposing weaknesses in regulatory oversight and raising questions about the credibility of auditors and analysts. The scandal also had significant financial implications, with investors in Wirecard losing billions of euros as the company's share price collapsed.

The scandal also had wider implications for the payments processing industry, which has grown rapidly in recent years as consumers have increasingly turned to digital and mobile payments. The scandal highlighted the need for greater transparency and accountability in the industry, particularly in relation to the handling of customer funds.

The scandal also led to increased scrutiny of the role of auditors in preventing and detecting financial fraud. The fact that Wirecard's auditors, EY, had signed off on the company's accounts for several years despite the mounting evidence of accounting irregularities raised serious questions about the effectiveness of the auditing process.

Wirecard also had a significant impact on the reputation of Germany's financial sector, which had previously been seen as relatively stable and well-regulated. The scandal led to criticism of the country's regulatory framework and sparked calls for reform to prevent similar incidents from happening in the future.

Specifics of the Wirecard Fraud:

- Wirecard was a German payment processing company that was once considered a tech unicorn and was listed on the German stock exchange.
- In 2020, it was revealed that Wirecard had a massive accounting scandal that involved over €1.9 billion in missing funds.
- The fraud was uncovered after the Financial Times published a series of articles that raised questions about Wirecard's accounting practices.
- Wirecard's CEO, Markus Braun, was arrested on charges of market manipulation and falsifying accounts. Other top executives were also implicated in the fraud.
- Wirecard's auditor, EY, also faced scrutiny for failing to detect the accounting irregularities. EY later acknowledged that it had failed to carry out proper auditing procedures and that there were "clear indications of fraudulent accounting."
- The scandal led to Wirecard filing for insolvency and being delisted from the stock exchange. It also resulted in numerous investigations by regulatory bodies and law enforcement agencies in Germany and around the world.

- The investigation uncovered a complex web of fraudulent transactions and fictitious assets created to inflate the company's revenue and profits. It involved a network of shell companies in Asia, including in the Philippines, Singapore, and Hong Kong.
- Wirecard allegedly used these shell companies to inflate revenue by processing fake transactions and then booking them as legitimate revenue. The company also allegedly created fictitious bank accounts to create the illusion of healthy balances.
- The fraud was reportedly going on for several years, with auditors and regulators failing to detect it despite multiple warnings and allegations of accounting irregularities.
- The Wirecard scandal is considered one of the largest accounting frauds in German corporate history, and it has raised questions about the effectiveness of corporate governance and auditing practices in the country.

"Sleight" is a gripping and informative read that delves deep into the world of corporate fraud. From Enron to Wirecard, this book provides a comprehensive overview of some of the biggest corporate scandals of the 21st century, and the lessons that can be learned from them.

As readers journey through these stories, they will gain valuable insight into the motivations and tactics of corporate fraudsters, and the devastating impact their actions can have on employees, shareholders, and the wider community.

Ultimately, "Sleight" is a call to action for greater transparency, accountability, and ethical conduct in the corporate world. By shining a light on these scandals, we can better understand how they occur and take steps to prevent them from happening in the future.

I hope that readers will find this book to be both informative and thought-provoking, and that it will inspire them to be vigilant and proactive in holding corporations to account. Thank you for taking the time to read "Sleight", and I hope that it will encourage meaningful dialogue and positive change in the corporate world.

END

Notes

Notes

Notes

Notes

Notes

Make the Best Use of The Book

1. Read actively: When reading, don't just passively absorb the information. Try to engage with the text by asking questions, making connections, and drawing conclusions.
2. Take notes: Jot down important points, quotes, and key ideas as you read. This will help you remember and retain the information better.
3. Reflect: After reading each chapter, take some time to reflect on what you've learned. Think about how you can apply the information in your own life.
4. Discuss with others: Engage in discussions with others about what you've read. This can help you gain new perspectives and insights.
5. Practice what you learn: Apply the lessons and ideas from the book in your daily life. Practice makes perfect, and the more you put into practice, the more you'll get out of the book.

Remember, the key to getting the best out of any book is to approach it with an open mind and a willingness to learn. Happy reading!

Motive

Dear reader,

I wrote "Sleight" with the intention of shedding light on the dark world of corporate fraud and the devastating consequences it can have on individuals and society as a whole. While researching and writing this book, I was struck by the depth and complexity of the frauds I encountered, as well as the tenacity and bravery of those who worked tirelessly to expose the truth.

As an author, I believe that it is my responsibility to use my platform to raise awareness of important issues and to spark conversations that can lead to positive change. My hope is that "Sleight" will not only inform and entertain, but also inspire readers to take a closer look at the systems and structures that allow corporate fraud to occur, and to demand greater accountability and transparency from those in power.

Thank you for taking the time to read "Sleight." I hope that this book will serve as a catalyst for important conversations and meaningful action.

Sincerely,

Sahil A Gosalia

About the Author

Sahil A Gosalia is a talented author who has a passion for writing and a deep interest in economics and finance. He has authored several books in the field of finance and economics, which reflect his expertise and knowledge of the subject.

Sahil's writing style is clear, concise, and engaging, making it easy for readers to understand complex financial concepts. He has a knack for breaking down complex financial topics into simple, understandable terms, which has helped readers gain a better understanding of the subject matter.

In addition to writing, Sahil is an avid reader of finance and economics books. He believes that knowledge is power and that reading is the best way to acquire knowledge. He spends a significant amount of time reading books and articles on finance and economics, which has helped him stay abreast of the latest developments and trends in the field.

Sahil is also a strong advocate for financial education and believes that everyone should have access to basic financial knowledge. He has dedicated his career to helping others understand finance and economics, and his books reflect this dedication.

Summary

"Sleight" is a riveting account of some of the most notorious cases of corporate fraud in recent history. Through meticulous research and compelling storytelling, the book explores the intricate and often hidden mechanisms of deceit that allowed these frauds to occur, from Enron to Steinhoff International to Wirecard.

Each chapter delves into the specifics of a different case, providing a detailed analysis of the key players, the methods used to commit the fraud, and the devastating consequences for investors, employees, and society at large.

Throughout the book, the reader is presented with a sobering reminder of the dangers of unchecked corporate power and the need for stronger regulations and oversight. "Sleight" is a must-read for anyone interested in the intersection of business and ethics, and a cautionary tale about the high stakes of corporate greed.

Scan to check more of my work!

Scan to BUY Books, Journals, Notebooks

Scan to BUY Kindle Edition E-Books

Scan to know more about the Author

www.ingramcontent.com/pod-product-compliance
Lightning Source LLC
Chambersburg PA
CBHW070754220526
45467CB00014B/423